Creating a coherent community

Ideal thoughts

By

Roshdy Ebrahim, Ph.D

2020

Roshdy Ebrahim

Copyright © 2020 Roshdy Ebrahim

All right reserved

Contents

Chapter 1

The revolutionary power of diverse thought [1]

"Can you taste words?" It was a question that caught me by surprise. This summer, I was giving a talk at a literary festival, and afterwards, as I was signing books, a teenage girl came with her friend, and this is what she asked me. I told her that some people experience an overlap in their senses so that they could hear colors or see sounds, and many writers were fascinated by this subject, myself included. But she cut me off, a bit impatiently, and said, "Yeah, I know all of that. It's called synesthesia. We learned it at school. But my mom is reading your book, and she says there's lots of food and ingredients and a long dinner scene in it. She gets hungry at every page. So, I was thinking, how come you don't get hungry when you write? And I thought maybe, maybe you could taste words. Does it make sense?"

And, actually, it did make sense, because ever since my childhood, each letter in the alphabet

____

)[1] shafak elif: Three Daughters of Eve, amazon, 2017

has a different color, and colors bring me flavors. So, for instance, the color purple is quite pungent, almost perfumed, and any words that I associate with purple taste the same way, such as "sunset" -- a very spicy word. But I was worried that if I tell all of this to the teenager, it might sound either too abstract or perhaps too weird, and there wasn't enough time anyhow, because people were waiting in the queue, so it suddenly felt like what I was trying to convey was more complicated and detailed than what the circumstances allowed me to say. And I did what I usually do in similar situations: I stammered, I shut down, and I stopped talking. I stopped talking because the truth was complicated, even though I knew, deep within, that one should never, ever remain silent for fear of complexity.

So, I want to start my talk today with the answer that I was not able to give on that day. Yes, I can taste words -- sometimes, that is, not always, and happy words have a different flavor than sad words. I like to explore: What does the word "creativity" taste like, or "equality," "love," "revolution?"

And what about "motherland?" These days, it's particularly this last word that troubles me. It leaves a sweet taste on my tongue, like cinnamon, a bit of rose water and golden apples. But underneath, there's a sharp tang, like nettles and dandelion. The taste of my motherland, Turkey, is a mixture of sweet and bitter.

And the reason why I'm telling you this is because I think there's more and more people all around the world today who have similarly mixed emotions about the lands they come from. We love our native countries, yeah? How can we not? We feel attached to the people, the culture, the land, the food. And yet at the same time, we feel increasingly frustrated by its politics and politicians, sometimes to the point of despair or hurt or anger.

I want to talk about emotions and the need to boost our emotional intelligence. I think it's a pity that mainstream political theory pays very little attention to emotions. Oftentimes, analysts and experts are so busy with data and metrics that they seem to forget those things in life that are difficult to measure and perhaps impossible to cluster under statistical models. But I think this is a mistake, for two main reasons. Firstly, because we are emotional beings. As human beings, I think we all are like that. But secondly, and this is new, we have entered a new stage in world history in which collective sentiments guide and misguide politics more than ever before. And through social media and social networking, these sentiments are further amplified, polarized, and they travel around the world quite fast. Ours is the age of anxiety, anger, distrust, resentment and, I think, lots of fear. But here's the thing: even though there's plenty of research about economic factors, there's relatively few studies about emotional factors.

Why is it that we underestimate feelings and perceptions? I think it's going to be one of our biggest intellectual challenges, because our political systems are replete with emotions. In country after country, we have seen illiberal politicians exploiting these emotions. And yet within the academia and among the intelligentsia, we are yet to take emotions seriously. I think we should. And just like we should focus on economic inequality worldwide, we need to pay more attention to emotional and cognitive gaps worldwide and how to bridge these gaps, because they do matter.

Years ago, when I was still living in Istanbul, an American scholar working on women writers in the Middle East came to see me. And at some point, in our exchange, she said, "I understand why you're a feminist, because, you know, you live in Turkey." And I said to her, "I don't understand why you're not a feminist, because, you know, you live in America."

And she laughed. She took it as a joke, and the moment passed. But the way she had divided the world into two imaginary camps, into two opposite camps -- it bothered me and it stayed with me. According to this imaginary map, some parts of the world were liquid countries. They were like choppy waters not yet settled. Some other parts of the world, namely the West, were solid, safe and stable. So, it was the liquid lands that needed feminism and activism and human rights, and those of us who were unfortunate enough to come from such places had to keep struggling for these most essential values. But there was hope. Since history moved forward, even the most unsteady lands would someday catch up. And meanwhile, the citizens of solid lands could take comfort in the progress of history and in the triumph of the liberal order. They could support the struggles of other people elsewhere, but they themselves did not have to struggle for the basics of democracy anymore, because they were beyond that stage.

I think in the year 2016, this hierarchical geography was shattered to pieces. Our world no longer follows this dualistic pattern in the scholar's mind, if it ever did. Now we know that history does not necessarily move forward. Sometimes it draws circles, even slides backwards, and that generations can make the same mistakes that their great-grandfathers had made. And now we know that there's no such thing as solid countries versus liquid countries. In fact, we are all living in liquid times, just like the late Zygmunt Bauman told us. And Bauman had another definition for our age. He used to say we are all going to be walking on moving sands.

And if that's the case, I think, it should concern us women more than men, because when societies slide backwards into authoritarianism, nationalism or religious fanaticism, women have much more to lose. That is why this needs to be a vital moment, not only for global activism, but in my opinion, for global sisterhood as well.

But I want to make a little confession before I go any further. Until recently, whenever I took part in an international conference or festival, I would be usually one of the more depressed speakers.

Having seen how our dreams of democracy and how our dreams of coexistence were crushed in Turkey, both gradually but also with a bewildering speed, over the years I've felt quite demoralized. And at these festivals there would be some other gloomy writers, and they would come from places such as Egypt, Nigeria, Pakistan, Bangladesh, Philippines, China, Venezuela, Russia. And we would smile at each other in sympathy, this camaraderie of the doomed.

And you could call us WADWIC: Worried and Depressed Writers International Club.

But then things began to change, and suddenly our club became more popular, and we started to have new members.

I remember Greek writers and poets joined first, came on board. And then writers from Hungary and Poland, and then, interestingly, writers from Austria, the Netherlands, France, and then writers from the UK, where I live and where I call my home, and then writers from the USA. Suddenly, there were more of us feeling worried about the fate of our nations and the future of the world. And maybe there were more of us now feeling like strangers in our own motherlands.

And then this bizarre thing happened. Those of us who used to be very depressed for a long time, we started to feel less depressed, whereas the newcomers, they were so not used to feeling this way that they were now even more depressed.

So, you could see writers from Bangladesh or Turkey or Egypt trying to console their colleagues from Brexit Britain or from post-election USA.

But joking aside, I think our world is full of unprecedented challenges, and this comes with an emotional backlash, because in the face of high-speed change, many people wish to slow down, and when there's too much unfamiliarity, people long for the familiar. And when things get too confusing, many people crave simplicity. This is a very dangerous crossroads, because it's exactly where the demagogue enters into the picture.

The demagogue understands how collective sentiments work and how he -- it's usually a he -- can benefit from them. He tells us that we all belong in our tribes, and he tells us that we will be safer if we are surrounded by sameness. Demagogues come in all sizes and in all shapes. This could be the eccentric leader of a marginal political party somewhere in Europe, or an Islamist extremist imam preaching dogma and hatred, or it could be a white supremacist Nazi-admiring orator somewhere else. All these figures, at first glance -- they seem disconnected. But I think they feed each other, and they need each other.

And all around the world, when we look at how demagogues talk and how they inspire movements, I think they have one unmistakable quality in common: they strongly, strongly dislike plurality. They cannot deal with multiplicity. Adorno used to say, "Intolerance of ambiguity is the sign of an authoritarian personality." But I ask myself: What if that same sign, that same intolerance of ambiguity -- what if it's the mark of our times, of the age we're living in? Because wherever I look, I see nuances withering away. On TV shows, we have one anti-something speaker situated against a pro-something speaker. Yeah? It's good ratings. It's even better if they shout at each other. Even in academia, where our intellect is supposed to be nourished, you see one atheist scholar competing with a firmly theist scholar, but it's not a real intellectual exchange, because it's a clash between two certainties.

I think binary oppositions are everywhere. So slowly and systematically, we are being denied the right to be complex. Istanbul, Berlin, Nice, Paris, Brussels, Dhaka, Baghdad, Barcelona: we have seen one horrible terror attack after another. And when you express your sorrow, and when you react against the cruelty, you get all kinds of reactions, messages on social media. But one of them is quite disturbing, only because it's so widespread. They say, "Why do you feel sorry for them? Why do you feel sorry for them? Why don't you feel sorry for civilians in Yemen or civilians in Syria?"

And I think the people who write such messages do not understand that we can feel sorry for and stand in solidarity with victims of terrorism and violence in the Middle East, in Europe, in Asia, in America, wherever, everywhere, equally and simultaneously. They don't seem to understand that we don't have to pick one pain and one place over all others. But I think this is what tribalism does to us. It shrinks our minds, for sure, but it also shrinks our hearts, to such an extent that we become numb to the suffering of other people.

And the sad truth is, we weren't always like this. I had a children's book out in Turkey, and when the book was published, I did lots of events. I went to many primary schools, which gave me a chance to observe younger kids in Turkey. And it was always amazing to see how much empathy, imagination and chutzpah they have. These children are much more inclined to become global citizens than nationalists at that age. And it's wonderful to see, when you ask them, so many of them want to be poets and writers, and girls are just as confident as boys, if not even more.

But then I would go to high schools, and everything has changed. Now nobody wants to be a writer anymore, now nobody wants to be a novelist anymore, and girls have become timid, they are cautious, guarded, reluctant to speak up in the public space, because we have taught them -- the family, the school, the society -- we have taught them to erase their individuality.

I think East and West, we are losing multiplicity, both within our societies and within ourselves. And coming from Turkey, I do know that the loss of diversity is a major, major loss. Today, my motherland became the world's biggest jailer for journalists, surpassing even China's sad record. And I also believe that what happened over there in Turkey can happen anywhere. It can even happen here. So just like solid countries was an illusion, singular identities are also an illusion, because we all have a multiplicity of voices inside. The Iranian, the Persian poet, Hafiz, used to say, "You carry in your soul every ingredient necessary to turn your existence into joy. All you have to do is to mix those ingredients."

And I think mix we can. I am an Istanbulite, but I'm also attached to the Balkans, the Aegean, the Mediterranean, the Middle East, the Levant. I am a European by birth, by choice, the values that I uphold. I have become a Londoner over the years. I would like to think of myself as a global soul, as a world citizen, a nomad and an itinerant storyteller. I have multiple attachments, just like all of us do. And multiple attachments mean multiple stories.

As writers, we always chase stories, of course, but I think we are also interested in silences, the things we cannot talk about, political taboos, cultural taboos. We're also interested in our own silences. I have always been very vocal about and written extensively about minority rights, women's rights, LGBT rights. I realized one thing: I have never had the courage to say in a public space that I was bisexual myself, because I so feared the slander and the stigma and the ridicule and the hatred that was sure to follow. But of course, one should never, ever, remain silent for fear of complexity.

And although I am no stranger to anxieties, and although I am talking here about the power of emotions -- I do know the power of emotions -- I have discovered over time that emotions are not limitless. You know? They have a limit. There comes a moment -- it's like a tipping point or a threshold -- when you get tired of feeling afraid, when you get tired of feeling anxious. And I think not only individuals, but perhaps nations, too, have their own tipping points. So even stronger than my emotions is my awareness that not only gender, not only identity, but life itself is fluid. They want to divide us into tribes, but we are connected across borders. They preach certainty, but we know that life has plenty of magic and plenty of ambiguity. And they like to incite dualities, but we are far more nuanced than that.

So, what can we do? I think we need to go back to the basics, back to the colors of the alphabet. The Lebanese poet Khalil Gibran used to say, "I learned silence from the talkative and tolerance from the intolerant and kindness from the unkind." I think it's a great motto for our times.

So, from populist demagogues, we will learn the indispensability of democracy. And from isolationists, we will learn the need for global solidarity. And from tribalists, we will learn the beauty of cosmopolitanism and the beauty of diversity.

I want to leave you with one word, or one taste. The word "yurt" in Turkish means "motherland." It means "homeland." But interestingly, the word also means "a tent used by nomadic tribes." And I like that combination, because it makes me think homelands do not need to be rooted in one place. They can be portable. We can take them with us everywhere. And I think for writers, for storytellers, at the end of the day, there is one main homeland, and it's called "Storyland." And the taste of that word is the taste of freedom.

Chapter 2

How we can face the future without fear [1]

"These are the times," said Thomas Paine, "that try men's souls." And they're trying ours now. This is a fateful moment in the history of the West. We've seen divisive elections and divided societies. We've seen a growth of extremism in politics and religion, all of it fueled by anxiety, uncertainty and fear, of a world that's changing almost faster than we can bear, and the sure knowledge that it's going to change faster still. I have a friend in Washington. I asked him, what was it like being in America during the recent presidential election? He said to me, "Well, it was like the man sitting on the deck of the Titanic with a glass of whiskey in his hand and he's saying, 'I know I asked for ice -- but this is ridiculous.'"

So, is there something we can do, each of us, to be able to face the future without fear? I think there is. And one way into it is to see that perhaps the simplest way into a culture and into an age is to

------

)[1] Jonathan sacks: Not in God's Name: Confronting Religious Violence. Amazon, 2015

ask: What do people worship? People have worshipped so many different things -- the sun, the stars, the storm. Some people worship many gods, someone, some none. In the 19th and 20th centuries, people worshipped the nation, the Aryan race, the communist state. What do we worship? I think future anthropologists will take a look at the books we read on self-help, self-realization, self-esteem. They'll look at the way we talk about morality as being true to oneself, the way we talk about politics as a matter of individual rights, and they'll look at this wonderful new religious ritual we have created. You know the one? Called the "selfie." And I think they'll conclude that what we worship in our time is the self, the me, the I.

And this is great. It's liberating. It's empowering. It's wonderful. But don't forget that biologically, we're social animals. We've spent most of our evolutionary history in small groups. We need those face-to-face interactions where we learn the choreography of altruism and where we create those spiritual goods like friendship and trust and loyalty and love that redeem our solitude. When we have too much of the "I" and too little of the "we," we can find ourselves vulnerable, fearful and alone. It was no accident that Sherry Turkle of MIT called the book she wrote on the impact of social media "Alone Together."

So, I think the simplest way of safeguarding the future "you" is to strengthen the future "us" in three dimensions: the us of relationship, the us of identity and the us of responsibility.

So, let me first take the us of relationship. And here, forgive me if I get personal. Once upon a time, a very long time ago, I was a 20-year-old undergraduate studying philosophy. I was into Nietzsche and Schopenhauer and Sartre and Camus. I was full of ontological uncertainty and existential angst. It was terrific.

I was self-obsessed and thoroughly unpleasant to know, until one day I saw across the courtyard a girl who was everything that I wasn't. She radiated sunshine. She emanated joy. I found out her name was Elaine. We met. We talked. We married. And 47 years, three children and eight grandchildren later, I can safely say it was the best decision I ever took in my life, because it's the people not like us that make us grow. And that is why I think we have to do just that.

The trouble with Google filters, Facebook friends and reading the news by narrowcasting rather than broadcasting means that we're surrounded almost entirely by people like us whose views, whose opinions, whose prejudices, even, are just like ours. And Cass Sunstein of Harvard has shown that if we surround ourselves with people with the same views as us, we get more extreme. I think we need to renew those face-to-face encounters with the people not like us. I think we need to do that in order to realize that we can disagree strongly and yet still stay friends. It's in those face-to-face encounters that we discover that the people not like us are just people, like us. And actually, every time we hold out the hand of friendship to somebody not like us, whose class or creed or color are different from ours, we heal one of the fractures of our wounded world. That is the us of relationship.

Second is the us of identity. Let me give you a thought experiment. Have you been to Washington? Have you seen the memorials? Absolutely fascinating. There's the Lincoln Memorial: Gettysburg Address on one side, Second Inaugural on the other. You go to the Jefferson Memorial, screeds of text. Martin Luther King Memorial, more than a dozen quotes from his speeches. I didn't realize, in America you read memorials. Now go to the equivalent in London in Parliament Square and you will see that the monument to David Lloyd George contains three words: David Lloyd George.

Nelson Mandela gets two. Churchill gets just one: Churchill. Why the difference? I'll tell you why the difference. Because America was from the outset a nation of wave after wave of immigrants, so it had to create an identity which it did by telling a story which you learned at school, you read on memorials and you heard repeated in presidential inaugural addresses. Britain until recently wasn't a nation of immigrants, so it could take identity for granted. The trouble is now that two things have happened which shouldn't have happened together. The first thing is in the West we've stopped telling this story of who we are and why, even in America. And at the same time, immigration is higher than it's ever been before. So when you tell a story and your identity is strong, you can welcome the stranger, but when you stop telling the story, your identity gets weak and you feel threatened by the stranger. And that's bad.

Jews have been scattered and dispersed and exiled for 2,000 years. We never lost our identity. Why? Because at least once a year, on the festival of Passover, we told our story and we taught it to our children and we ate the unleavened bread of affliction and tasted the bitter herbs of slavery. So, we never lost our identity. I think collectively we've got to get back to telling our story, who we are, where we came from, what ideals by which we live. And if that happens, we will become strong enough to welcome the stranger and say, "Come and share our lives, share our stories, share our aspirations and dreams." That is the us of identity.

And finally, the us of responsibility. Do you know something? My favorite phrase in all of politics, very American phrase, is: "We the people." Why "we the people?" Because it says that we all share collective responsibility for our collective future. And that's how things really are and should be.

Have you noticed how magical thinking has taken over our politics? So, we say, all you've got to do is elect this strong leader and he or she will solve all our problems for us. Believe me, that is magical thinking. And then we get the extremes: the far right, the far left, the extreme religious and the extreme anti-religious, the far right dreaming of a golden age that never was, the far left dreaming of a utopia that never will be and the religious and anti-religious equally convinced that all it takes is God or the absence of God to save us from ourselves. That, too, is magical thinking, because the only people who will save us from ourselves is, we the people, all of us together. And when we do that, and when we move from the politics of me to the politics of all of us together, we rediscover those beautiful, counterintuitive truths: that a nation is strong when it cares for the weak, that it becomes rich when it cares for the poor, it becomes invulnerable when it cares about the vulnerable. That is what makes great nations.

So here is my simple suggestion. It might just change your life, and it might just help to begin to change the world. Do a search and replace operation on the text of your mind, and wherever you encounter the word "self," substitute the word "other." So instead of self-help, other-help; instead of self-esteem, other-esteem. And if you do that, you will begin to feel the power of what for me is one of the most moving sentences in all of religious literature. "Though I walk through the valley of the shadow of death, I will fear no evil, for you are with me." We can face any future without fear so long as we know we will not face it alone.

So, for the sake of the future "you," together let us strengthen the future "us."

Chapter 3

Why the only future worth building includes everyone? [1]

As I meet, or lend an ear to those who are sick, to the migrants who face terrible hardships in search of a brighter future, to prison inmates who carry a hell of pain inside their hearts, and to those, many of them young, who cannot find a job, I often find myself wondering: "Why them and not me?" I, myself, was born in a family of migrants; my father, my grandparents, like many other Italians, left for Argentina and met the fate of those who are left with nothing. I could have very well ended up among today's "discarded" people. And that's why I always ask myself, deep in my heart: "Why them and not me?"

First and foremost, I would love it if this meeting could help to remind us that we all need each other, none of us is an island, an autonomous and independent "I," separated from the other, and we can only build the future by standing together,

------

)[1] Pope francis: bishop of Rome.

including everyone. We don't think about it often, but everything is connected, and we need to restore our connections to a healthy state. Even the harsh judgment I hold in my heart against my brother or my sister, the open wound that was never cured, the offense that was never forgiven, the rancor that is only going to hurt me, are all instances of a fight that I carry within me, a flare deep in my heart that needs to be extinguished before it goes up in flames, leaving only ashes behind.

Many of us, nowadays, seem to believe that a happy future is something impossible to achieve. While such concerns must be taken very seriously, they are not invincible. They can be overcome when we don't lock our door to the outside world. Happiness can only be discovered as a gift of harmony between the whole and each single component. Even science – and you know it better than I do – points to an understanding of reality as a place where every element connects and interacts with everything else.

And this brings me to my second message. How wonderful would it be if the growth of scientific and technological innovation would come along with more equality and social inclusion. How wonderful would it be, while we discover faraway planets, to rediscover the needs of the brothers and sisters orbiting around us. How wonderful would it be if solidarity, this beautiful and, at times, inconvenient word, were not simply reduced to social work, and became, instead, the default attitude in political, economic and scientific choices, as well as in the relationships among individuals, peoples and countries. Only by educating people to a true solidarity will we be able to overcome the "culture of waste," which doesn't concern only food and goods but, first and foremost, the people who are cast aside by our techno-economic systems which, without even realizing it, are now putting products at their core, instead of people.

Solidarity is a term that many wishes to erase from the dictionary. Solidarity, however, is not an automatic mechanism. It cannot be programmed or controlled. It is a free response born from the heart of each and everyone. Yes, a free response! When one realizes that life, even in the middle of so many contradictions, is a gift, that love is the source and the meaning of life, how can they withhold their urge to do good to another fellow being?

In order to do good, we need memory, we need courage and we need creativity. Yes, love does require a creative, concrete and ingenious attitude. Good intentions and conventional formulas, so often used to appease our conscience, are not enough. Let us help each other, all together, to remember that the other is not a statistic or a number. The other has a face. The "you" is always a real presence, a person to take care of.

There is a parable Jesus told to help us understand the difference between those who'd rather not be bothered and those who take care of the other. I am sure you have heard it before. It is the Parable of the Good Samaritan. When Jesus was asked: "Who is my neighbor?" - namely, "Who should I take care of?" - he told this story, the story of a man who had been assaulted, robbed, beaten and abandoned along a dirt road. Upon seeing him, a priest and a Levite, two very influential people of the time, walked past him without stopping to help. After a while, a Samaritan, a very much despised ethnicity at the time, walked by. Seeing the injured man lying on the ground, he did not ignore him as if he weren't even there. Instead, he felt compassion for this man, which compelled him to act in a very concrete manner. He poured oil and wine on the wounds of the helpless man, brought him to a hostel and paid out of his pocket for him to be assisted.

The story of the Good Samaritan is the story of today's humanity. People's paths are riddled with suffering, as everything is centered around money, and things, instead of people. And often there is this habit, by people who call themselves "respectable," of not taking care of the others, thus leaving behind thousands of human beings, or entire populations, on the side of the road. Fortunately, there are also those who are creating a new world by taking care of the other, even out of their own pockets. Mother Teresa actually said: "One cannot love, unless it is at their own expense."

We have so much to do, and we must do it together. But how can we do that with all the evil we breathe every day? Thank God, no system can nullify our desire to open up to the good, to compassion and to our capacity to react against evil, all of which stem from deep within our hearts. Now you might tell me, "Sure, these are beautiful words, but I am not the Good Samaritan, nor Mother Teresa of Calcutta." On the contrary: we are precious, each and every one of us. Each and every one of us is irreplaceable in the eyes of God. Through the darkness of today's conflicts, each and every one of us can become a bright candle, a reminder that light will overcome darkness, and never the other way around.

To Christians, the future does have a name, and its name is Hope. Feeling hopeful does not mean to be optimistically naïve and ignore the tragedy humanity is facing. Hope is the virtue of a heart that doesn't lock itself into darkness, that doesn't dwell on the past, does not simply get by in the present, but is able to see a tomorrow. Hope is the door that opens onto the future. Hope is a humble, hidden seed of life that, with time, will develop into a large tree. It is like some invisible yeast that allows the whole dough to grow, that brings flavor to all aspects of life. And it can do so much, because a tiny flicker of light that feeds on hope is enough to shatter the shield of darkness. A single individual is enough for hope to exist, and that individual can be you. And then there will be another "you," and another "you," and it turns into an "us." And so, does hope begin when we have an "us?" No. Hope began with one "you." When there is an "us," there begins a revolution.

The third message I would like to share today is, indeed, about revolution: the revolution of tenderness. And what is tenderness? It is the love that comes close and becomes real. It is a movement that starts from our heart and reaches the eyes, the ears and the hands. Tenderness means to use our eyes to see the other, our ears to hear the other, to listen to the children, the poor, those who are afraid of the future. To listen also to the silent cry of our common home, of our sick and polluted earth. Tenderness means to use our hands and our heart to comfort the other, to take care of those in need.

Tenderness is the language of the young children, of those who need the other. A child's love for mom and dad grows through their touch, their gaze, their voice, their tenderness. I like when I hear parents talk to their babies, adapting to the little child, sharing the same level of communication. This is tenderness: being on the same level as the other. God himself descended into Jesus to be on our level. This is the same path the Good Samaritan took. This is the path that Jesus himself took. He lowered himself, he lived his entire human existence practicing the real, concrete language of love.

Yes, tenderness is the path of choice for the strongest, most courageous men and women. Tenderness is not weakness; it is fortitude. It is the path of solidarity, the path of humility. Please, allow me to say it loud and clear: the more powerful you are, the more your actions will have an impact on people, the more responsible you are to act humbly. If you don't, your power will ruin you, and you will ruin the other. There is a saying in Argentina: "Power is like drinking gin on an empty stomach." You feel dizzy, you get drunk, you lose your balance, and you will end up hurting yourself and those around you, if you don't connect your power with humility and tenderness. Through humility and concrete love, on the other hand, power – the highest, the strongest one – becomes a service, a force for good.

The future of humankind isn't exclusively in the hands of politicians, of great leaders, of big companies. Yes, they do hold an enormous responsibility. But the future is, most of all, in the hands of those people who recognize the other as a "you" and themselves as part of an "us." We all need each other. And so, please, think of me as well with tenderness, so that I can fulfill the task I have been given for the good of the other, of each and every one, of all of you, of all of us.

Chapter 4

Reducing violence in cities [1]

You are a trauma surgeon, working in the midnight shift in an inner-city emergency room. A young man is wheeled in before you, lying unconscious on a gurney. He's been shot in the leg and is bleeding profusely. Judging from the entry and exit wounds, as well as the amount of hemorrhaging, the bullet most likely clipped the femoral artery, one of the largest blood vessels in the body. As the young man's doctor, what should you do? Or more precisely, what should you do first?

You look at the young man's clothes, which seem old and worn. He may be jobless, homeless, lacking a decent education. Do you start treatment by finding him a job, getting him an apartment or helping him earn his GED? On the other hand, this young man has been involved in some sort of conflict and may be dangerous. Before

____

)[1] Thomas Abt: Bleeding Out: The Devastating Consequences of Urban Violence--and a Bold New Plan for Peace in the Streets, amazon 2019

he wakes up, do you place him in restraints, alert hospital security or call 911? Most of us wouldn't do any of these things. And instead, we would take the only sensible and humane course of action available at the time. First, we would stop the bleeding. Because unless we stop the bleeding, nothing else matters.

What's true in the emergency room is true for cities all around the country. When it comes to urban violence, the first priority is to save lives. Treating that violence with the same urgency that we would treat a gunshot wound in the ER. What are we talking about when we say "urban violence"? Urban violence is the lethal or potentially lethal violence that happens on the streets of our cities. It goes by many names: street violence, youth violence, gang violence, gun violence. Urban violence happens among the most disadvantaged and disenfranchised among us. Mostly young men, without a lot of options or much hope.

I have spent hundreds of hours with these young men. I've taught them at a high school in

Washington DC, where one of my students was murdered. I've stood across form them in courtrooms in New York City, where I worked as a prosecutor. And finally, I've gone from city to city as a policymaker and as a researcher, meeting with these young men and exchanging ideas on how to make our communities safer. Why should we care about these young men? Why does urban violence matter?

Urban violence matters, because it causes more deaths here in the United States than any other form of violence. Urban violence also matters because we can actually do something about it. Controlling it is not the impossible, intractable challenge that many believe it to be. In fact, there are a number of solutions available today that are proven to work. And what these solutions have in common is one key ingredient. They all recognize that urban violence is sticky, meaning that its clusters together among a surprisingly small number of people and places.

In New Orleans, for instance, a network of fewer than 700 individuals account for the majority of the city's lethal violence. Some call these individuals "hot people." Here in Boston, 70 percent of shootings are concentrated on blocks and corners covering just five percent of the city. These locations are often known as "hot spots." In city after city, a small number of hot people and hot spots account for the clear majority of lethal violence. In fact, this finding has been replicated so many times that researchers now call this phenomenon the law of crime concentration.

When we look at the science, we see that sticky solutions work best. To put it bluntly, you can't stop shootings if you won't deal with shooters. And you can't stop killings if you won't go where people get killed.

Four years ago, my colleagues and I performed a systematic meta-review of antiviolence strategies, summarizing the results of over 1,400 individual impact evaluations. What we found, again and again, was that the strategies that were the most focused, the most targeted, the stickiest strategies, were the most successful. We saw this in criminology, in studies of policing, gang prevention and reentry. But we also saw this in public health, where targeted tertiary and secondary prevention performed better than more generalized primary prevention. When policymakers focus on the most dangerous people and places, they get better results.

What about replacement and displacement, you might ask. Research shows that when drug dealers are locked up, new dealers' step right in, replacing those that came before. Some worry that when police focus on certain locations, crime will be displaced, moving down the street or around the corner. Fortunately, we know now that because of the stickiness phenomenon, the replacement and displacement effects associated with these sticky strategies are minimal. It takes a lifetime of trauma to create a shooter and decades of disinvestment to create a hot spot. So, these people and places don't move around easily.

What about root causes? Isn't addressing poverty or inequality or lack of opportunity the best way to prevent violence? Well, according to the science, yes and no. Yes, in that high rates of violence are clearly associated with various forms of social and economic disadvantage. But no, in that changes in these factors do not necessarily result in changes in violence, especially not in the short run. Take poverty, for instance. Meaningful progress on poverty will take decades to achieve, while poor people need and deserve relief from violence right now. Root causes also can't explain the stickiness phenomenon. If poverty always drove violence, then we would expect to see violence among all poor people. But we don't see that.

Instead, we can empirically observe that poverty concentrates, crime concentrates further still and violence concentrates most of all. That is why sticky solutions work. They work, because they deal with first things first. And this is important, because while poverty may lead to violence, strong evidence shows that violence actually perpetuates poverty.

Here's just one example of how. As documented by Patrick Sharkey, a sociologist -- he showed that when poor children are exposed to violence, it traumatizes them. It impacts their ability to sleep, to pay attention, to behave and to learn. And if poor children can't learn, then they can't do well in school. And that ultimately impacts their ability to earn a paycheck later in life that is large enough to escape poverty.

And unfortunately, in a series of landmark studies by economist Raj Chetty, that is exactly what we've seen. Poor children exposed to violence have lower income mobility than poor children who grow up peacefully. Violence literally traps poor kids in poverty. That is why it is so important to focus relentlessly on urban violence. Here are two examples of how.

Here in Boston, in the 1990s, a partnership between cops and community members achieved a stunning 63 percent reduction in youth homicide. In Oakland, that same strategy recently reduced nonfatal gun assaults by 55 percent. In Cincinnati, Indianapolis and New Haven, it cut gun violence by more than a third. At its simplest, this strategy simply identifies those who are most likely to shoot or be shot, and then confronts them with a double message of empathy and accountability. "We know it's you that's doing the shooting. It must stop. If you let us, we will help you. If you make us, we will stop you." Those willing to change are offered services and support. Those who persist in their violent behavior are brought to justice via targeted law enforcement action.

In Chicago, another program uses cognitive behavioral therapy to help teenage boys manage difficult thoughts and emotions, by teaching them how to avoid or mitigate conflicts. This program reduced violent crime arrests among participants by half. Similar strategies have reduced criminal reoffending by 25 to 50 percent. Now Chicago has launched a new effort, using these same techniques, but with those at the highest risk for gun violence. And the program is showing promising results. What's more, because these strategies are so focused, so targeted, they tend not to cost much in absolute terms. And they work with the laws already on the books today.

So that's the good news. We can have peace in our cities, right now, without big budgets and without new laws. So why hasn't this happened yet? Why are these solutions still limited to a small number of cities, and why do they struggle, even when successful, to maintain support? Well, that's the bad news. The truth is, we have not been very good at organizing our efforts around this phenomenon of stickiness.

There are at least three reasons why we don't follow the evidence when it comes to urban violence reduction. And the first, as you might expect, is politics. Most sticky solutions don't conform to one political platform or another. Instead, they offer both carrots and sticks, balancing the promise of treatment with the threat of arrest, combining place-based investment with hot-spots policing. In other words, these solutions are both soft and tough at the same time. Because they don't line up neatly with the typical talking points of either the Left or the Right, politicians won't gravitate to these ideas without some education, and maybe even a little pressure. It won't be easy, but we can change the politics around these issues by reframing violence as a problem to be solved, not an argument to be won. We should emphasize evidence over ideology and what works versus what sounds good.

The second reason why we don't always follow the evidence is the somewhat complicated nature of these solutions. There is an irony here. What are the simplest ways to reduce violence? More cops. More jobs. Fewer guns. These are easy to spell out, but they tend not to work as well in practice. While on the other hand, research-based solutions are harder to explain, but get better results. Right now, we have a lot of professors writing about violence in academic journals. And we have a lot of people keeping us safe out on the street. But what we don't have is a lot of communication between these two groups. We don't have a strong bridge between research and practice. And when research actually does inform practice, that bridge is not built by accident. It happens when someone takes the time to carefully explain what the research means, why it's important and how it can actually make a difference in the field. We spend plenty of time creating research, but not enough breaking it down into bite-sized bits that a busy cop or social worker can easily digest.

It may be difficult to acknowledge or accept, but race is the third and final reason why more has not been done to reduce violence. Urban violence concentrates among poor communities of color. That makes it easy for those of us who don't live in those communities to ignore the problem or pretend it's not ours to solve. That is wrong, of course. Urban violence is everyone's problem. Directly or indirectly, we all pay a price for the shootings and killings that happen on the streets of our cities. That is why we need to find new ways to motivate more people to cross class and color lines to join this struggle. Because these strategies are not resource-intensive, we don't need to motivate many new allies -- we just need a few. And we just need them to be loud.

If we can overcome these challenges and spread these sticky solutions to the neighborhoods that need them, we could save thousands of lives. If the strategies I've discussed here today were implemented right now in the nation's 40 most violent cities, we could save over 12,000 souls over the next eight years.

How much would it cost? About 100 million per year. That might sound like a lot, but in fact, that figure represents less than one percent of one percent of the annual federal budget. The Defense Department spends about that much for a single F-35 fighter jet.

Metaphorically, the treatment is the same, whether it's a young man suffering from a gunshot wound, a community riddled with such wounds, or a nation filled with such communities. In each case, the treatment, first and foremost, is to stop the bleeding. I know this can work. I know it, because I've seen it. I've seen shooters put down their guns and devote their lives to getting others to do the same. I've walked through housing projects that were notorious for gunfire and witnessed children playing outside. I've sat with cops and community members who used to hate one another, but now work together. And I've seen people from all walks of life, people like you, finally decide to get involved in this struggle. And that's why I know that together, we can and we will end this senseless slaughter.

Chapter 5 Helping young people build a better future [1]

Today, there are 1.8 billion young people between the ages of 10 and 24 in the world. It is the largest cohort in human history. Meeting their needs will be a big challenge. But it's also a big opportunity.

They hold our shared future in their hands. Every day, we read about young people lending their ideas and passions to fighting for change, social change, political change, change in their communities. Imagine what they'll create: breakthroughs, inventions. Maybe new medicines, new modes of transportation, new ways to communicate, sustainable economies and maybe even a world at peace. But this opportunity, this youth dividend, is not a given.

One point eight billion young women and young men are standing at the door of adulthood. Are they ready? Right now, too few of them are. My favorite part of my job at UNICEF is

____

)[1] Henrietta fore: child advocate

a chance to talk to, meet with and hear from young people all around the world. And they tell me about their hopes and dreams. And they have amazing hopes and dreams for what they'll accomplish in their lives. But what they're also telling me is that they have fears.

They feel that they're facing a series of urgent crises. A crisis of demographics, a crisis of education, a crisis of employment, a crisis of violence and a crisis for girls. If you look at these crises, you realize that they're urgent and they need to be addressed now. Because they tell us that they're worried. They're worried that they might not get the education that they need. And you know what? They're right.

Two hundred million adolescents are out of school worldwide, about the population of Brazil. And those that are in school feel that they may not be getting the right skills. Globally, six in 10 children and young people do not meet the minimum proficiency level for reading and mathematics. No country can be successful if nearly half of its population of young people are unable to read or write. And what about the lucky few who are in secondary school? Many of them are dropping out because they're worried that they're not getting skills that they can use to make a livelihood. And sometimes, their parents can no longer afford the fees. It's a tragedy.

And young people are also telling me that they're worried about employment, that they won't be able to find a job. And again, they're right. Every month, 10 million young people reach working age. It's a staggering number. Some will go on for further education, but many will enter the workforce. And our world is not creating 10 million new jobs each month. The competition is fierce for the jobs that are available. So, imagine being a young person today, needing a job, seeking a livelihood, ready to build a future, and opportunities are hard to find.

Young people are also telling me that they're worried that they're not getting the skills that they need. And again, they're right. We are finding ourselves at a time in the world when the world is changing so fast for work. We're in the fourth industrial revolution. Young people do not want to be on the farms and in rural communities. They want to go to the cities. They want to learn future skills for future work. They want to learn digital technology and green technologies. They want to have a chance to learn modern agriculture. They want to learn business and entrepreneurship, so that they can create a business of their own. They want to be nurses and radiologists and pharmacists and doctors. And they want to have all of the skills that they'll need for the future. They also want to learn the trades, like construction and electricians. These are all the professions that a country needs, as well as the professions that have not been invented yet.

And young people are also telling me that they're worried about violence. At home, online, in school, in their communities. And again, they're right. A young person can have hundreds of friends on social media, but when they need to find a friendly face, someone who can be there as their friend, to talk to, they do not find one. They face bullying, harassment and more. And hundreds of millions are facing exploitation and abuse, and violence. Every seven minutes, an adolescent boy or girl somewhere in the world is killed by an act of violence.

And girls are telling me that they're especially worried about their futures. And sadly, they're right, too. Girls face prejudice and discrimination. They face early childhood marriage and they face life-threatening early pregnancy. Imagine a population of the United States. Now double it. That's the number of women who were married before their 18th birthday. Six hundred and fifty million. And many were mothers while they were still children themselves. One out of every three women will face physical abuse or sexual abuse in her lifetime. So, no wonder girls are worried about their futures.

These urgent crises may not be a reality in your life or in your neighborhood. And perhaps you've had opportunities for a good education and for marketable skills, and for getting a job. And maybe you've never faced violence, or prejudice, or discrimination. But there are tens of millions of young people who are not so lucky. And they are sounding the alarm for their futures.

And that is why UNICEF and our many public and private partners are launching a new global initiative. Young people themselves have named it. And it's called Generation Unlimited or Gen-U or Gen you. So, what they're saying is, it's our time, it's our turn, it's our future.

Our goal is very straightforward. We want every young person in school, learning, training, or age-appropriate employment by the year 2030. This goal is urgent, it's necessary, it's ambitious. But we think it's also achievable. So, we're calling out for cutting-edge solutions and new ideas. Ideas that will give young people a fighting chance for their futures. We don't know all the answers, so we're reaching out to businesses and governments, and nonprofits, and academia, and communities, and innovators for help.

Gen-U is to be an open platform, where people can come and share their ideas and solutions about what works, what does not work, and importantly, what might work. So, if we can take these ideas and add a little bit of seed money, and add some good partners, and add good political will, we think they can scale up to reach thousands and millions of people around the world. And with this project, we're also going to do something new. We're going to co-design and co-create with young people. So, with Gen-U, they're going to be in the driver's seat, steering us all along the way.

In Argentina, there's a program where we connect students who are in rural, remote, hard to reach mountainous communities, with something they've seldom seen: a secondary school teacher. So these students come to a classroom, they're joined by a community teacher and they're connected to urban schools online. And there is the secondary school teacher, who is teaching them about digital technology and a good secondary school education, without them ever having to leave their own communities.

And in South Africa, there's a program called Techno Girls. And these are girls from disadvantaged neighborhoods who are studying the STEM program area: science, technology, engineering and math. And they have a chance to job shadow. This is the way that they then can see themselves in jobs that are in engineering, in science, and maybe in the space program.

In Bangladesh, we have partners who are training tens of thousands of young people in the trades, so that they can become motorcycle repair people, or mobile phone service people. But these are a chance to see their own livelihoods. And maybe even to have a business of their own.

And in Vietnam, there's a program where we are pairing young entrepreneurs with the needs in their own local communities. So, with this program, a group gathered and they decided that they would solve the problem of transportation for people with disabilities in their communities. So, with a mentor and a bit of seed funding, they've now developed a new app to help the whole community.

And I've seen how these programs can make a difference. When I was in Lebanon, I visited a program called Girls Got IT, or Girls Got It. And in this program, girls who have been studying computer skills and the STEM program have a chance to work side by side with young professionals, so that they can learn firsthand what it's like to be an architect, a designer or a scientist. And when you see these girls, smiles on their faces, the hot lights in their eyes, they are so excited, they have hope for the future. They want to change the world. And now, with this program and these mentors, they'll be able to do it.

But these ideas and programs are just a start. They'll only reach a fraction of the young people that we need to reach. We want to take these ideas and find ways to scale them up. To reach more young people in more communities, in more places around the world. And we want to dream big. Could every school, everywhere in the world, no matter how remote or mountainous, or even if it's in a refugee camp, could they be connected to the internet? Could we have instant translation for young people, so that you could get a good education in your own language, anywhere in the world? And would it be possible that we could connect the education in your school with skills that you're going to need to get a job in your own community? So that you actually can move from school to work. And more.

Can each one of us help? In our everyday lives and in our workplaces, are there ways that we could support young people? Young people are asking us for apprenticeships, for job shadowing, for internships. Could we do this? Young people are also asking us for work-study programs, places where they can learn and earn. Could we do this and could we reach out to a community that's nearby, that's less advantaged, and help them? Young people are also saying that they want to help other young people. They want more space and more voice, so that they can gather to help each other. In HIV centers, in refugee camps, but also to stop online bullying and early child marriage.

We need ideas, we need ideas that are big and small, ideas that are local and global. This, in the end, is our responsibility. A massive generation of young people are about to inherit our world. It is our duty to leave a legacy of hope and opportunity for them but also with them. Young people are 25 percent of our population. But they are 100 percent of our future. And they're calling out for a fighting chance to build a better world. So, their call should be our calling. The calling of our time. The time is now, the need is urgent. And 1.8 billion young people are waiting.

Chapter 6 The political power of being a good neighbor [1]

I know for sure there's at least one thing I have in common with dentists. I absolutely hate the holiday of Halloween. Now, this hatred stems not from a dislike of cavities, nor was it a lifetime in the making. Rather, this hatred stems from a particular incident that happened nine years ago.

Nine years ago, I was even younger, I was 20 years old, and I was an intern in the White House. The other White House. And my job was to work with mayors and councilors nationwide. November 1, 2010 began just like any other day. I turned on the computer, went on Google and prepared to write my news clips. I was met with a call from my mother, which isn't that out the norm, my mom likes to text, call, email, Facebook, Instagram, all that. So, I answered the phone expecting to hear maybe some church gossip, or maybe something from World Star HipHop she had discovered. But when I answered the phone, I was

---

)[1] Michael Tubbs: mayor of the city of Stockton, California

met with a tone that was unlike anything I had ever heard from my mother. My mother's loud. But she spoke in a hush, still, muffled tone that conveyed a sense of sadness. And as she whispered, she said, "Michael, your cousin Donnell was murdered last night, on Halloween, at a house party in Stockton."

And like far too many people in this country, particularly from communities like mine, particularly that look like me, I spent the better part of the year dealing with anger, rage, nihilism, and I had a choice to make. The choice was one between action and apathy. The choice was what could I do to put purpose to this pain. I spent a year dealing with feelings of survivor's guilt. What was the point of me being at Stanford, what was the point of me being at the White House if I was powerless to help my own family? And my own family was dying, quite literally. I then began to feel a little selfish and say, what's the point of even trying to make the world a better place? Maybe that's just the way it is. Maybe I would be smart to take advantage of all the opportunities given to me and make as much money as possible, so I'm comfortable, and my immediate family is comfortable.

But finally, towards the end of that year, I realized I wanted to do something. So, I made the crazy decision, as a senior in college, to run for city council. That decision was unlikely for a couple of reasons, and not just my age. You see, my family is far from a political dynasty. More men in my family have been incarcerated than in college. In fact, as I speak today, my father is still incarcerated. My mother, she had me as a teenager, and government wasn't something we had warm feelings from. You see, it was the government that red-lined the neighborhoods I grew up in. Full of liquor stores and no grocery stores, there was a lack of opportunity and concentrated poverty. It was the government and the politicians that made choices, like the war on drugs and three strikes, that have incarcerated far too many people in our country. It was the government and political actors that made the decisions that created the school funding formulas, that made it so the school I went to receive less per pupil spending than schools in more affluent areas. So, there was nothing about that background that made it likely for me to choose to be involved in being a government actor.

And at the same time, Stockton was a very unlikely place. Stockton is my home town, a city of 320,000 people. But historically, it's been a place people run from, rather than come back to. It's a city that's incredibly diverse. Thirty-five percent Latino, 35 percent white, 20 percent Asian, 10 percent African American, the oldest Sikh temple in North America. But at the time I ran for office, we were also the largest city in the country at that time to declare bankruptcy. At the time I decided to run for office, we also had more murders per capita than Chicago. At the time I decided to run for office, we had a 23 percent poverty rate, a 17 percent college attainment rate and a host of challenges and issues beyond the scope of any 21-year-old.

So, after I won my election, I did what I usually do when I feel overwhelmed, I realized the problems of Stockton were far bigger than me and that I might need a little divine intervention. So as I prepared for my first council meeting, I went back to some wisdom my grandmother taught me. A parable I think we all know, that really constitutes the governing frame we're using to reinvent Stockton today.

I remember in Sunday school, my grandmother told me that at one time, a guy asked Jesus, "Who was my neighbor? Who was my fellow citizen? Who am I responsible for?" And instead of a short answer, Jesus replied with a parable. He said there was a man on a journey, walking down Jericho Road. As he was walking down the road, he was beat up, left on the side of the road, stripped of all his clothes, had everything stolen from and left to die. And then a priest came by, saw the man on the side of the road, maybe said a silent prayer, hopes and prayers, prayers that he gets better. Maybe saw the man on the side of the road and surmised that it was ordained by God for this particular man, this particular group to be on the side of the road, there's nothing I can do to change it.

After the priest walked by, maybe a politician walked by. A 28-year-old politician, for example. Saw the man on the side of the road and saw how beat up the man was, saw that the man was a victim of violence, or fleeing violence. And the politician decided, "You know what? Instead of welcoming this man in, let's build a wall. Maybe the politician said, "Maybe this man chose to be on the side of the road." That if he just pulled himself up by his bootstraps, despite his boots being stolen, and got himself back on the horse, he could be successful, and there's nothing I could do." And then finally, my grandmother said, a good Samaritan came by, saw the man on the side of the road and looked and saw not centuries of hatred between Jews and Samaritans, looked and saw not his fears reflected, not economic anxiety, not "what's going to happen to me because things are changing." But looked and saw a reflection of himself. He saw his neighbor; he saw his common humanity. He didn't just see it, he did something about it, my grandmother said. He got down on one knee, he made sure the man was OK, and I heard, even gave him a room at that nice Fairmont, the Pan Pacific one.

And as I prepared to govern, I realized that given the diversity of Stockton, the first step to making change will be to again answer the same question: Who is our neighbor? And realizing that our destiny as a city was tied up in everyone. Particularly those who are left on the side of the road. But then I realized that charity isn't justice, that acts of empathy isn't justice, that being a good neighbor is necessary but not sufficient, and there was more that had to be done. So, looking at the story, I realized that the road, Jericho Road, has a nickname. It's known as the Bloody Pass, the Ascent of Red, because the road is structured for violence. This Jericho Road is narrow, it's conducive for ambushing. Meaning, a man on the side of the road wasn't abnormal. Wasn't strange. And in fact, it was something that was structured to happen, it was supposed to happen.

And Johan Galtung, a peace theorist, talks about structural violence in our society. He says, "Structural violence is the avoidable impairment of basic human needs." Dr. Paul Farmer talks about structural violence and talks about how it's the way our institutions, our policies, our culture creates outcomes that advantage some people and disadvantage others. And then I realized, much like the road in Jericho, in many ways, Stockton, our society, has been structured for the outcomes we complain about. That we should not be surprised when we see that kids in poverty don't do well in school, that we should not be surprised to see wealth gaps by race and ethnicity. We should not be surprised to see income pay disparities between genders, because that's what our society, historically, has been structured to do, and it's working accordingly.

So, taking this wisdom, I rolled up my sleeves and began to work. And there's three quick stories I want to share, that point to not that we figured everything out, not that we have arrived, but we're trending in the right direction. The first story, about the neighbor. When I was a city council member, I was working with one of the most conservative members in our community on opening a health clinic for undocumented people in the south part of the city, and I loved it. And as we opened the clinic, we had a resolution to sign, he presented me a gift. It was an O'Reilly Factor lifetime membership pin.

Mind you, I didn't ask what he did to get such a gift. What blood oath -- I had no idea how he got it. But I looked at him and I said, "Well, how are we working together to open a health clinic, to provide free health care for undocumented people, and you're an O'Reilly Factor member?" He looked at me and said, "Councilman Tubbs, this is for my neighbors." And he's a great example of what it means to be a good neighbor, at least in that instance.

The robbers. So, after four years on city council, I decided to run for mayor, realizing that being a part-time councilman wasn't enough to enact the structural changes we need to see in Stockton, and I came to that conclusion by looking at the data. So, my old council district, where I grew up, is 10 minutes away from a more affluent district. And 10 minutes away in the same city, the difference between zip code 95205 and 95219 in life expectancy is 10 years. Ten minutes away, 4.5

miles, 10 years life expectancy difference, and not because of the choices people are making. Because no one chose to live in an unsafe community where they can't exercise. No one chose to put more liquor stores than grocery stores in the community. No one chose these things, but that's the reality. I realized, as a councilman, to enact a structural change I wanted to see, where between the same zip codes there's a 30 percent difference in the rate of unemployment, there's 75,000 dollars a year difference in income, that being a councilman was not going to cut it. So that's when I decided to run for mayor.

And as mayor, we've been focused on the robbers and the road. So, in Stockton, as I mentioned, we have historically had problems with violent crime. In fact, that's why I decided to run for office in the first place. And my first job as mayor was helping our community to see ourselves, our neighbors, not just in the people victimized by violence but also in the perpetrators. We realized that those who enact pain in our society, those who are committing homicides and contributing to gun violence, are oftentimes victims themselves. They have high rates of trauma, they have been shot at, they've known people who have been shot. That doesn't excuse their behavior, but it helps explain it, and as a community, we have to see these folks as us, too. That they too are our neighbors. So, for the past three years we've been working on two strategies: Ceasefire and Advance Peace, where we give these guys as much attention, as much love from social services, from opportunities, from tattoo removals, in some cases even cash, as a gift from law enforcement. And last year, we saw a 40 percent reduction in homicides and a 30 percent reduction in violent crime.

And now, the road. I mentioned that my community has a 23 percent poverty rate. As someone who comes from poverty, it's a personal issue for me. So, I decided that we wouldn't just do a program, or we wouldn't just do something to go around the edges, but we would call into question the very structure that produces poverty in the first place. So, starting in February, we launched a basic income demonstration, where for the next 18 months, as a pilot, 130 families, randomly selected, who live in zip codes at or below the median income of the city, are given 500 dollars a month. And we're doing this for a couple of reasons. We're doing it because we realize that something is structurally wrong in America, when one in two Americans can't afford one 400-dollar emergency. We're doing it because we realize that something is structurally wrong when wages have only increased six percent between 1979 and 2013. We're doing it because we realize something is structurally wrong when people working two and three jobs, doing all the jobs no one in here wants to do, can't pay for necessities, like rent, like lights, like health care, like childcare.

So, I would say, Stockton again, we have real issues. I have constituent emails in my phone now, about the homelessness issue, about some of the violent crime we're still experiencing. But I would say, I think as a society, we would be wise to go back to those old Bible stories we were taught growing up, and understand that number one, we have to begin to see each other as neighbors, that when we see someone different from us, they should not reflect our fears, our anxieties, our insecurities, the prejudices we've been taught, our biases -- but we should see ourselves. We should see our common humanity. Because I think once we do that, we can do the more important work of restructuring the road.

Because again, I understand some listening are saying, "Well, Mayor Tubbs, you're talking about structural violence and structural this, but you're on the stage. That the structures can't be too bad if you could come up from poverty, have a father in jail, go to Stanford, work in the White House and become mayor." And I would respond by saying the term for that is exceptionalism. Meaning that we recognize it's exceptional for people to escape the structures. Meaning by our very language, we understand that the things we're seeing in our world are by design. And I think that task for us, as TEDsters, and as good people, just people, moral people, is really do the hard work necessary of not just joining hands as neighbors, but using our hands to restructure our road, a road that in this country has been rooted in things like white supremacy. A road like in this country has been rooted in things like misogyny. A road that's not working for far too many people. And I think today, tomorrow and 2020 we have a chance to change that.

So, as I prepare to close, I started with a story from nine years ago and I'll end with one. So, after my cousin was murdered, I was lucky enough to go on the Freedom Rides with some of the original freedom riders. And they taught me a lot about restructuring the road. And one guy in particular, Bob Singleton, asked me a question I'm going to leave with us today. We were going to Anniston, Alabama, and he said, "Michael," and I said, "Yes, sir."

He said, "I was arrested on August 4, 1961. Now why is that day important?" And I said, "Well, you were arrested, if you weren't arrested, we wouldn't be on this bus. if we weren't on this bus, we wouldn't have the rights we enjoy."

He rolled his eyes and said, "No, son." He said, "On that day, Barack Obama was born." And then he said he had no idea that the choice he made to restructure the road would pave the way, so a child born as a second-class citizen, who wouldn't be able to even get a cup of water at a counter, would have the chance, 50 years later, to be president.

Then he looked at me and he said, "What are you prepared to do today so that 50 years from now a child born has a chance to be president?" And I think, that's the question before us today. We know things are jacked up. I think what we've seen recently isn't abnormal but a reflection of a system that's been structured to produce such crazy outcomes. But I think it's also an opportunity. Because these structures we inherit aren't acts of God but acts of men and women, they're policy choices, they're by politicians like me, approved by voters like you. And we have the chance and the awesome opportunity to do something about it.

So, my question is: What are we prepared to do today, so that a child born today, 50 years from now isn't born in a society rooted in white supremacy; isn't born into a society riddled with misogyny; isn't born into a society riddled with homophobia and transphobia and anti-Semitism and Islamophobia and ableism, and all the phobias and -

isms? What are we prepared to do today, so that 50 years from now we have a road in our society that's structured to reflect what we hold to be self-evident? That all men, that all women, that even all trans people are created equal and are endowed by your Creator with certain unalienable rights, including life, liberty and the pursuit of happiness.

Chapter 7

The new power of collaboration [1]

biology is war in which only the fiercest survive; businesses and nations succeed only by defeating, destroying and dominating competition; politics is about your side winning at all costs. But I think we can see the very beginnings of a new story beginning to emerge. It's a narrative spread across a number of different disciplines, in which cooperation, collective action and complex interdependencies play a more important role. And the central, but not all-important, role of competition and survival of the fittest shrinks just a little bit to make room.

I started thinking about the relationship between communication, media and collective action when I wrote "Smart Mobs," and I found that when I finished the book, I kept thinking about it. In fact, if you look back, human communication media and the ways in which we organize socially have been co-evolving for quite a long

---

)[1] Howard Rheingold: digital community builder

time. Humans have lived for much, much longer than the approximately 10,000 years of settled agricultural civilization in small family groups. Nomadic hunters bring down rabbits, gathering food. The form of wealth in those days was enough food to stay alive. But at some point, they banded together to hunt bigger game. And we don't know exactly how they did this, although they must have solved some collective action problems; it only makes sense that you can't hunt mastodons while you're fighting with the other groups.

And again, we have no way of knowing, but it's clear that a new form of wealth must have emerged. More protein than a hunter's family could eat before it rotted. So that raised a social question that I believe must have driven new social forms. Did the people who ate that mastodon meat owe something to the hunters and their families? And if so, how did they make arrangements? Again, we can't know, but we can be pretty sure that some form of symbolic communication must have been involved.

Of course, with agriculture came the first big civilizations, the first cities built of mud and brick, the first empires. And it was the administers of these empires who began hiring people to keep track of the wheat and sheep and wine that was owed and the taxes that was owed on them by making marks; marks on clay in that time.

Not too much longer after that, the alphabet was invented. And this powerful tool was really reserved, for thousands of years, for the elite administrators (Laughter) who kept track of accounts for the empires. And then another communication technology enabled new media: the printing press came along, and within decades, millions of people became literate. And from literate populations, new forms of collective action emerged in the spheres of knowledge, religion and politics. We saw scientific revolutions, the Protestant Reformation, constitutional democracies possible where they had not been possible before. Not created by the printing press, but enabled by the collective action that emerges from literacy. And again, new forms of wealth emerged.

Now, commerce is ancient. Markets are as old as the crossroads. But capitalism, as we know it, is only a few hundred years old, enabled by cooperative arrangements and technologies, such as the joint-stock ownership company, shared liability insurance, double-entry bookkeeping.

Now of course, the enabling technologies are based on the Internet, and in the many-to-many era, every desktop is now a printing press, a broadcasting station, a community or a marketplace. Evolution is speeding up. More recently, that power is untethering and leaping off the desktops, and very, very quickly, we're going to see a significant proportion, if not the majority of the human race, walking around holding, carrying or wearing supercomputers linked at speeds greater than what we consider to be broadband today.

Now, when I started looking into collective action, the considerable literature on it is based on what sociologists' call "social dilemmas." And there are a couple of mythic narratives of social dilemmas. I'm going to talk briefly about two of them: the prisoner's dilemma and the tragedy of the commons.

Now, when I talked about this with Kevin Kelly, he assured me that everybody in this audience pretty much knows the details of the prisoner's dilemma, so I'm just going to go over that very, very quickly. If you have more questions about it, ask Kevin Kelly later.

The prisoner's dilemma is actually a story that's overlaid on a mathematical matrix that came out of the game theory in the early years of thinking about nuclear war: two players who couldn't trust each other. Let me just say that every unsecured transaction is a good example of a prisoner's dilemma. Person with the goods, person with the money, because they can't trust each other, are not going to exchange. Neither one wants to be the first one or they're going to get the sucker's payoff, but both lose, of course, because they don't get what they want. If they could only agree, if they could only turn a prisoner's dilemma into a different payoff matrix called an assurance game, they could proceed.

Twenty years ago, Robert Axelrod used the prisoner's dilemma as a probe of the biological question: if we are here because our ancestors were such fierce competitors, how does cooperation exist at all? He started a computer tournament for people to submit prisoner's dilemma strategies and discovered, much to his surprise, that a very, very simple strategy won -- it won the first tournament, and even after everyone knew it won, it won the second tournament -- that's known as tit for tat.

Another economic game that may not be as well-known as the prisoner's dilemma is the ultimatum game, and it's also a very interesting probe of our assumptions about the way people make economic transactions. Here's how the game is played: there are two players; they've never played the game before, they will not play the game again, they don't know each other, and they are, in fact, in separate rooms. First player is offered a hundred dollars and is asked to propose a split: 50/50, 90/10, whatever that player wants to propose. The second player either accepts the split -- both players are paid and the game is over -- or rejects the split -- neither player is paid and the game is over.

Now, the fundamental basis of neoclassical economics would tell you it's irrational to reject a dollar because someone you don't know in another room is going to get 99. Yet in thousands of trials with American and European and Japanese students, a significant percentage would reject any offer that's not close to 50/50. And although they were screened and didn't know about the game and had never played the game before, proposers seemed to innately know this because the average proposal was surprisingly close to 50/50.

Now, the interesting part comes in more recently when anthropologists began taking this game to other cultures and discovered, to their surprise, that slash-and-burn agriculturalists in the Amazon or nomadic pastoralists in Central Asia or a dozen different cultures -- each had radically different ideas of what is fair. Which suggests that instead of there being an innate sense of fairness, that somehow the basis of our economic transactions can be influenced by our social institutions, whether we know that or not.

The other major narrative of social dilemmas is the tragedy of the commons. Garrett Hardin used it to talk about overpopulation in the late 1960s. He used the example of a common grazing area in which each person by simply maximizing their own flock led to overgrazing and the depletion of the resource. He had the rather gloomy conclusion that humans will inevitably despoil any common pool resource in which people cannot be restrained from using it.

Now, Elinor Ostrom, a political scientist, in 1990 asked the interesting question that any good scientist should ask, which is: is it really true that humans will always despoil commons? So, she went out and looked at what data she could find. She looked at thousands of cases of humans sharing watersheds, forestry resources, fisheries, and discovered that yes, in case after case, humans destroyed the commons that they depended on. But she also found many instances in which people escaped the prisoner's dilemma; in fact, the tragedy of the commons is a multiplayer prisoner's dilemma. And she said that people are only prisoners if they consider themselves to be. They escape by creating institutions for collective action. And she discovered, I think most interestingly, that among those institutions that worked, there were a number of common design principles, and those principles seem to be missing from those institutions that don't work.

I'm moving very quickly over a number of disciplines. In biology, the notions of symbiosis, group selection, evolutionary psychology are contested, to be sure. But there is really no longer any major debate over the fact that cooperative arrangements have moved from a peripheral role to a central role in biology, from the level of the cell to the level of the ecology. And again, our notions of individuals as economic beings have been overturned. Rational self-interest is not always the dominating factor. In fact, people will act to punish cheaters, even at a cost to themselves.

And most recently, neurophysiological measures have shown that people who punish cheaters in economic games show activity in the reward centers of their brain. Which led one scientist to declare that altruistic punishment may be the glue that holds societies together.

Now, I've been talking about how new forms of communication and new media in the past have helped create new economic forms. Commerce is ancient. Markets are very old. Capitalism is fairly recent; socialism emerged as a reaction to that. And yet we see very little talk about how the next form may be emerging. Jim Surowiecki briefly mentioned Yochai Benkler's paper about open source, pointing to a new form of production: peer-to-peer production. I simply want you to keep in mind that if in the past, new forms of cooperation enabled by new technologies create new forms of wealth, we may be moving into yet another economic form that is significantly different from previous ones.

Very briefly, let's look at some businesses. IBM, as you know, HP, Sun -- some of the fiercest competitors in the IT world are open sourcing their software, are providing portfolios of patents for the commons. Eli Lilly -- in, again, the fiercely competitive pharmaceutical world -- has created a market for solutions for pharmaceutical problems. Toyota, instead of treating its suppliers as a marketplace, treats them as a network and trains them to produce better, even though they are also training them to produce better for their competitors. Now none of these companies are doing this out of altruism; they're doing it because they're learning that a certain kind of sharing is in their self-interest.

Open source production has shown us that world-class software, like Linux and Mozilla, can be created with neither the bureaucratic structure of the firm nor the incentives of the marketplace as we've known them. Google enriches itself by enriching thousands of bloggers through AdSense. Amazon has opened its Application Programming Interface to 60,000 developers, countless Amazon shops. They're enriching others, not out of altruism but as a way of enriching themselves. eBay solved the prisoner's dilemma and created a market where none would have existed by creating a feedback mechanism that turns a prisoner's dilemma game into an assurance game.

Instead of, "Neither of us can trust each other, so we have to make suboptimal moves," it's, "You prove to me that you are trustworthy and I will cooperate." Wikipedia has used thousands of volunteers to create a free encyclopedia with a million and a half articles in 200 languages in just a couple of years.

We've seen that Think Cycle has enabled NGOs in developing countries to put up problems to be solved by design students around the world, including something that's being used for tsunami relief right now: it's a mechanism for rehydrating cholera victims that's so simple to use it, illiterates can be trained to use it. BitTorrent turns every downloader into an uploader, making the system more efficient the more it is used.

Millions of people have contributed their desktop computers when they're not using them to link together through the Internet into supercomputing collectives that help solve the

protein folding problem for medical researchers --
that's Folding @home at Stanford -- to crack codes,
to search for life in outer space.

I don't think we know enough yet. I don't
think we've even begun to discover what the basic
principles are, but I think we can begin to think
about them. And I don't have enough time to talk
about all of them, but think about self-interest. This
is all about self-interest that adds up to more. In El
Salvador, both sides that withdrew from their civil
war took moves that had been proven to mirror a
prisoner's dilemma strategy.

In the U.S., in the Philippines, in Kenya,
around the world, citizens have self-organized
political protests and get out the vote campaigns
using mobile devices and SMS. Is an Apollo Project
of cooperation possible? A transdisciplinary study
of cooperation? I believe that the payoff would be
very big. I think we need to begin developing maps
of this territory so that we can talk about it across
disciplines. And I am not saying that understanding
cooperation is going to cause us to be better people
-- and sometimes people cooperate to do bad things

-- but I will remind you that a few hundred years ago, people saw their loved ones die from diseases they thought were caused by sin or foreigners or evil spirits.

Descartes said we need an entire new way of thinking. When the scientific method provided that new way of thinking and biology showed that microorganisms caused disease, suffering was alleviated. What forms of suffering could be alleviated, what forms of wealth could be created if we knew a little bit more about cooperation? I don't think that this transdisciplinary discourse is automatically going to happen; it's going to require effort. So, I enlist you to help me get the cooperation project started.

Chapter 8 Effective tech to connect communities in crisis [1]

I'm an immigrant from Venezuela, and I've lived in the US for six years. If you ask me about my life as an expatriate, I would say that I've been lucky. But it hasn't been easy.

Growing up, I never thought that I was going to leave my homeland. I participated in my first student protest in 2007, when the president shut down one of the most important news networks. I was getting my bachelor's degree in communications, and that was the first time I realized I couldn't take free speech for granted.

We knew things were getting bad, but we never saw what was coming: an economic crisis, infrastructure breaking down, citywide electrical blackouts, the decline of public health care and shortage of medicines, disease outbreaks and starvation. I moved to Canada with my husband in 2013, and we always thought we'd move back home when the crisis improved. But we never did. Nearly

---

)[1] Johanna Figueira: digital marketing consultant

all my childhood friends have left the country, but my parents are still there. There have been moments where I've called my mom, and I could hear people screaming and crying in the background as teargas bombs exploded in the streets. And my mom, as if I couldn't hear it, would always tell me,

"We're fine, don't worry." But of course, I worry. It's my parents, and I'm 4,000 miles away.

Today, I'm just one of more than four million Venezuelans who have left their home country. A lot of my friends are Venezuelan immigrants, and in the last few years, we've begun talking about how we could make a difference when we live so far away. That is how Code for Venezuela was born in 2019.

It began with a hackathon, because we are experts in tech, and we thought we could use our tech skills to create solutions for people on the ground. But first, we needed to find some experts actually living inside Venezuela to guide us. We'd see so many other hackathons that came up with wily, ambitious, incredible technological solutions that sounded great in theory but ultimately failed to work in the actual countries they were intended to help. Many of us have been living abroad for years, and we are detached from the day-to-day problems that people are facing in Venezuela. So we turned to the experts actually living inside of the country.

For example, Julio Castro, a doctor and one of the leaders of Médicos por la Salud. When the government stopped publishing official health care data in 2015, Dr. Julio began collecting information himself, using an informal but coordinated system of cell phone communications. They track available personnel, medical supplies, mortality data, disease outbreaks; compile it into a report; and then share that on Twitter. He became our go-to expert on health care in Venezuela.

Luis Carlos Díaz, a widely recognized journalist who reports acts of censorship and human rights violations suffered by the people of Venezuela, he helps us make sense of what is happening there, since the news is controlled by the government.

We call these people our heroes on the ground. With their expert advice, we came up with a series of challenges for hackathon participants. In that first hackathon, we had 300 participants from seven countries come up with 16 different project submissions. We picked the projects with the most potential and continued working on them after the event. Today, I'll share two of our most successful projects to give you a taste of the impact we are having so far. They're called MediTweet and Blackout Tracker.

MediTweet is an intelligent Twitter bot that helps Venezuelans find the medicine they need. Right now, in Venezuela, if you get sick and you go to a hospital, there is a good chance they won't have the right medical supplies to treat you. The situation is so bad that patients often get a "shopping list" from the doctor instead of a prescription.

I live the need for this firsthand. My mom was diagnosed with cancer in 2015. She needed to have a lumbar puncture to get a final diagnosis and treatment plan. But the needle for this procedure wasn't available. I was in Venezuela at that time, and I was seeing my mom getting worse in front of me every day. After looking everywhere, we found the needle in a site that is like the eBay of Latin America. I met the seller in a local bakery, and it was like buying something on the black market. My mom brought the needle to her doctor, and he did the procedure. Without this, she could have died.

But it's not just medical supplies, it's medicines, too. When she was first diagnosed, we bought her treatment in a state pharmacy, and it was, like, practically free. But then the state pharmacy ran out, and we still had six months of treatment ahead. Six months of treatment ahead. We bought some medicines online and the rest in Mexico. Now she's in her third year of remission, and every time that I call, she tells me, "I'm fine, don't worry."

But not everyone can afford to leave the country, and many aren't healthy enough to travel. That is why people turn to Twitter, buying and selling medicines using the hashtag

#ServicioPublico, meaning "public service." Our Twitter bot scans Twitter for the hashtag #ServicioPublico and connects users who are asking for specific medicines with those who are selling their private leftovers. We also pool the location data of those Twitter users and use it for a visualization tool. It gives local organizations like Médicos por la Salud a sense of where they have a shortage. We can also apply machine learning algorithms to detect clusters of disease. If they've received humanitarian aid, this could help them to make better decisions about the distributions of the supplies.

Our second project, is called Blackout Tracker. Venezuela is currently going through an electricity crisis. Last year, Venezuela suffered what some people consider the worst power failures in Venezuelan history. I had two long days without communication with my parents. Some cities experienced blackouts every day. But you only know about this on social media. The government won't report blackouts on the news. When the power goes out, many Venezuelans, we quickly tweet out the location with the hashtag

#SinLuz, meaning "without electricity," before their phones ran out of battery, so people around the country know what is happening. Like MediTweet, Blackout Tracker scans Twitter for the hashtag #SinLuz and creates a map using the location data of those users. You can quickly see where the blackouts are happening today and how many blackouts have happened over time.

People want to know what is happening, and this is our answer. But it's also a way of holding the government accountable. It's easy for them to deny that the problem exists or make excuses, because there is no official data on it. Blackout Tracker shows how bad the problem really is.

Now, some people in Silicon Valley may look at these projects and say that there are no major technological innovations. But that is the point. These projects are not insanely advanced, but it's what the people of Venezuela need, and they can have a tremendous impact. Beyond these projects, perhaps our most significant accomplishment is that a movement has been created, one where people around the world are coming together to use their professional skills to create solutions for the people of Venezuela. And because we are partnering with locals, we are creating the solutions that people want and need.

What is so great about this is that we are using our professional skills, so it comes easily and naturally. It's not that hard for us to make a difference. If someone from San Francisco were to hire professionals to create solutions like MediTweet or Blackout Tracker, it would cost a small fortune. By donating our services, we are making a bigger impact than if we were just to donate money.

And you can do the same thing -- not in Venezuela, necessarily, but in your own community. In a world that is more connected than ever, we still see how specialized communities can be living isolated or in silos. There are so many great ways to help, but I believe that you can use your professional skills to connect diverse communities and create effective solutions through those relationships.

Anyone with knowledge and professional skills has a powerful force to bring hope to a community. For us at Code for Venezuela, this is just the beginning.

Chapter 9

Finding common ground [1]

our story started several years ago, when my wife and I got a complaint letter in the mail from an anonymous neighbor. I'll never forget the way my wife transformed before my eyes from this graceful, peaceful, sweet woman into just an angry mother grizzly bear whose cubs needed to be protected. It was intense. So, here's what happened.

We have five awesome kids. We're pretty loud, we're pretty rambunctious, we're us. though, that two of our children look a little different than Mary and I, and that's because they came to us through adoption. Our neighbor, though, saw two different-looking children playing outside of our house every day and came to the conclusion that we must have been running an illegal day care out of our home.

We were really angry to have our children stereotyped like that, but I know that's a relatively minor example of racial profiling. But isn't it

---

)[1] Matt Trombley: Maven, teacher, team builder

sometimes what we all tend to do with people who think differently, or believe differently or maybe even vote differently? Instead of engaging as true neighbors, we keep our distance and our actions towards those are guided by who we think sees the world as we do or who we think doesn't.

See, what my neighbor suffered from is a condition called agonism. And sometimes we all suffer from the same condition. It's not a medical condition, but it is contagious. So, let's talk a little bit about what agonism is. My favorite definition of agonism is taking a warlike stance in contexts that are not literally war. Agonism comes from the same Greek root word "agon" from which we get "agony." How very appropriate. We all tend to show symptoms of agonism when we hold on to two deeply held beliefs, first identified by author Rick Warren. The first one is that if love someone, we must agree with all they do or believe. And the second is the inverse, that if we disagree with someone, it must mean that we fear or we hate them.

Not sure we really recognize the agony this way of thinking brings to us, when our relationships die because we think we have to agree or disagree no matter what. Think about the conversations we've had around Brexit, or Hong Kong, maybe Israeli settlements or perhaps impeachment. I bet we could all think of at least one personal relationship that's been strained or maybe even ended because of these topics, or tragically, over a topic much more trivial than those. The cure for agonism is not out of reach. The question is how.

So, might I suggest two strategies that my experience has taught me to start with. First, cultivate common ground, which means focusing on what we share. I want you to know I'm using my words very, very deliberately. By "cultivate," I mean we have to intentionally work to find common ground with someone. Just like a farmer works to cultivate the soil. And common ground is a common term, so let me at least explain what I don't mean, which is I don't mean by common ground that we were exact, or that we totally agree and approve. All I mean is that we find one unifying thing that we can have in a relationship in common with another person.

You know, sometimes that one thing is hard to find. So, I'd like to share a personal story, but before I do, let me tell you a little bit more about myself. I'm Caucasian, cisgender male, middle class, evangelical Christian. And I know, as soon as some of those words came out of my mouth, some of you had some perceptions about me. And it's OK, I know that not all those perceptions are positive. But for those who share my faith, know that I'm about to cut across the grain. And you may tune me out as well. So, as we go, if you're having a hard time hearing me, I just gently ask that you reflect and see if you're buying into agonism. If you're rejecting me simply because you think you see the world differently than I do, because isn't that what we're here talking about? Alright, ready?

So, I've been thinking a lot about how to find common ground in the area of gender fluidity, as an evangelical Christian. For Christians like me, we believe that God created us man and woman. So, what do I do? Do I throw up my hands and say, "I can't have a relationship with anybody who is transgender or LGBTQIA?" No. That would be giving into agonism.

So, I started looking at the foundational aspects of my faith, the first of which is that of the three billion genes that make us human -- and by the way, we share 99.9 percent of those genes -- that I believe those three billion genes are the result of an intelligent designer. And that immediately gives me common ground with anybody. What it also gives me ... is the belief that each and every one of us have been given the right to life by that same intelligent designer.

I dug deeper though. I found that my faith didn't teach me to start relationships by arguing with somebody until they believed what I believed, or I convinced them. No, it taught me to start relationships by loving them as a coequal member of the human race. Honestly though, some who share my faith draw a line and refuse to address somebody by their preferred gender pronoun. But isn't that believing the lie that in order for me to honor you, I have to give up what I believe?

Come back in time with me -- let's say it's 20 years ago, and Muhammad Ali comes to your doorstep. And you open the door. Would you address him as Muhammad Ali or his former name of Cassius Clay? I'm guessing that most of you would say Muhammad Ali. And I'm also guessing that most of you wouldn't think we'd have to immediately convert to Islam, just by using his name. To honor him would cost me, would cost any of us absolutely nothing, and it would give us the common ground to have a relationship. And it's the relationship that cures agonism, not giving up what we believe.

So, for me to honor my faith, it means rejecting these rigid symptoms of agonism. Meaning, I can and I will love you. I can and I will accept you, and I don't have to buy into the lie that if I do these things, I have to give up what I believe or chose to fear and hate you. Because I'm focusing on what we have in common.

When you can find even the smallest bit of common ground with somebody, it allows you to understand just the beautiful wonder and complexity and majesty of the other person.

Our second strategy gives us room to (Inhales) breathe. To pause. To calm down. To have the kind of relationships that cure agonism. And how to keep those relationships alive. Our second strategy is to exchange extravagant grace. Once again, I'm not mincing words -- by grace, I don't mean we should all go sign up for ballet, that would be weird.

What I mean is not canceling everything over one mistake. Even if that mistake personally offended you. Maybe even deeply. Perhaps Holocaust survivor Corrie ten Boom put it best when she said, "To forgive is to set a prisoner free, only to realize that prisoner was me." My faith teaches me that we humans will never be perfect, myself very much included. So, we need the grace of a savior, who for me is Jesus. And while I define grace in the context of my faith, I know there's a lot of other people who have defined it differently and in different ways. One of my favorites is radio broadcaster Oswald Hoffmann, who said, "Grace is the love that loves the unlovely and the unlovable." And I just love that picture of grace. Because I know I am, and maybe a lot of you can think of a time when we're just pretty dadgum unlovable.

So, it would be the height of hypocrisy, dare I say repulsive to my faith, for me to accept the unconditional, unqualified grace and love from God and then turn around and put one precondition on the love I give you. What in the world would I be thinking? And by extravagant, I mean over the top, not just checking a box. We can all remember when we were kids and our parents forced us to apologize to somebody and we walked up to them and said, (Angrily) "I'm sorry." We just got it over with, right? That's not what we're talking about. What we're talking about is not having to give someone grace but choosing to and wanting to. That's how we exchange extravagant grace.

Listen, I know this can sound really, really theoretical. So, I'd like to tell you about a hero of mine. A hero of grace. It's 2014. In Iran. And the mother of a murdered son is in a public square. The man who murdered her son is also in that square, by gallows, on a chair of some kind, a noose around his neck and a blindfold over his eyes. Samereh Alinejad had been given the sole right under the laws of her country to either pardon this man or initiate his execution. Put another way, she could pardon him or literally push that chair out from underneath his feet.

I just ... I can't picture the agony going through both Samereh and this man at the time. Samereh with her choice to make, and this man, in the account that I read, was just weeping, just begging for forgiveness. And Samereh had a choice. And she chose in that moment to walk up to this man and to slap him right across the face. And that signaled her pardon. It gets better.

Right afterwards, somebody asked her, they interviewed her, and she was quoted as saying, "I felt as if rage vanished from within my heart and the blood in my veins began to flow again." Isn't that incredible? I mean, what a picture of grace, what a hero of grace. And there's a lesson in there for all of us. That as theologian John Piper said, "Grace is power, not just pardon." And if you think about it, grace is the gift we give someone else in a relationship that says our relationship is way more important than the things that separate us. And if you really think about it some more, we all have the power to execute in our relationships, or to pardon.

We never did find out the identity of our anonymous neighbor. But if we did, I'd hope we'd simply say, "Can we have coffee?" And maybe there's somebody you need to have coffee with and find your common ground with them. Or maybe there's somebody you're in a relationship with and you need to exchange extravagant grace. Maybe go first.

These two strategies have taught me how to exchange extravagant grace in my relationships and to enjoy the beautiful design of my neighbors. I want to continue to choose relationships over agonism. Will you choose to join me?

Chapter 10

Urban spaces can preserve history and build community [1]

How can landscapes imbue memory? When we think about this notion "e pluribus unum" -- "out of many, one," it's a pretty strange concept, right? I mean, with all different races and cultures of people, how do you boil it down to one thing? I want to share with you today this idea of "e pluribus unum" and how our landscape might imbue those memories of diverse perspectives, as well as force us to stop trying to narrow things down to a single, clean set of identities.

As an educator, designer, I'd like to share with you five simple concepts that I've developed through my work. And I'd like to share with you five projects where we can begin to see how the memory around us, where things have happened, can actually force us to look at one another in a different way. And lastly: this is not

____

)[1] Walter hood: creative director

just an American motto anymore. I think e pluribus unum is global. We're in this thing together.

First, great things happen when we exist in each other's world -- like today, right? The world of community gardens -- most of you have probably seen a community garden. They're all about subsistence and food. Right? I'll tell you a little story, what happened in New York more than a decade ago. They tried to sell all of their community gardens, and Bette Midler developed a nonprofit, the New York Restoration Project. They literally brought all the gardens and decided to save them. And then they had another novel idea: let's bring in world-class designers and let them go out into communities and make these beautiful gardens, and maybe they might not just be about food. And so, they called me, and I designed one in Jamaica, Queens. And on the way to designing this garden, I went to the New York Restoration Project Office, and I noticed a familiar name on the door downstairs. I go upstairs, and I said, "Do you guys know who is downstairs?" And they said, "Gunit." And I said, "Gunit? You mean G-Unit? Curtis '50 Cent' Jackson?"

And so we went downstairs, and before you knew it, Curtis, Bette and the rest of them formed this collaboration, and they built this garden in Jamaica, Queens. And it turned out Curtis, 50 Cent, grew up in Jamaica. And so again, when you start bringing these worlds together -- me, Curtis, Bette -- you get something more incredible. You get a garden that last year was voted one of the top 10 secret gardens in New York. Right?

It's for young and old, but more importantly, it's a place -- there was a story in the Times about six months ago where this young woman found solace in going to the garden. It had nothing to do with me. It had more to do with 50, I'm sure, but it has inspired people to think about gardens and sharing each other's worlds in a different way.

This next concept, "two-ness" -- it's not as simple as I thought it would be to explain, but as I left to go to college, my father looked at me, and said, "Junior, you're going to have to be both black and white when you go out there." And if you go back to the early parts of the 20th century, W.E.B.

Du Bois, the famous activist, said it's this peculiar sensation that the Negro has to walk around being viewed through the lens of other people, and this two-ness, this double consciousness. And I want to argue that more than a hundred years later, that two-ness has made us strong and resilient, and I would say for brown people, women -- all of us who have had to navigate the world through the eyes of others -- we should now share that strength to the rest of those who have had the privilege to be singular.

I'd like to share with you a project, because I do think this two-ness can find itself in the world around us. And it's beginning to happen where we're beginning to share these stories. At the University of Virginia, the academical village by Thomas Jefferson, it's a place that we're beginning to notice now was built by African hands. So, we have to begin to say, "OK, how do we talk about that?" As the University was expanding to the south, they found a site that was the house of Kitty Foster, free African American woman. And she was there, and her descendants, they all lived there, and she cleaned for the boys of UVA. But as they found the archaeology, they asked me if I would do a commemorative piece. So, the two-ness of this landscape, both black and white ... I decided to do a piece based on shadows and light. And through that, we were able to develop a shadow-catcher that would talk about this two-ness in a different way. So, when the light came down, there would be this ride to heaven. When there's no light, it's silent. And in the landscape of Thomas Jefferson, it's a strange thing. It's not made of brick. It's a strange thing, and it allows these two things to be unresolved.

And we don't have to resolve these things. I want to live in a world where the resolution -- there's an ambiguity between things, because that ambiguity allows us to have a conversation. When things are clear and defined, we forget.

The next example? Empathy. And I've heard that a couple of times in this conference, this notion of caring. Twenty-five years ago, when I was a young pup, very optimistic, we wanted to design a park in downtown Oakland, California for the homeless people. And we said, homeless people can be in the same space as people who wear suits. And everyone was like, "That's never going to work. People are not going to eat lunch with the homeless people."

We built the park. It cost 1.1 million dollars. We wanted a bathroom. We wanted horseshoes, barbecue pits, smokers, picnic tables, shelter and all of that. We had the design, we went to the then-mayor and said, "Mr. Mayor, it's only going to cost you 1.1 million dollars." And he looked at me. "For homeless people?" And he didn't give us the money.

So, we walked out, unfettered, and we raised the money. Clorox gave us money. The National Park Service built the bathroom. So, we were able to go ahead because we had empathy.

Now, 25 years later, we have an even larger homeless problem in the Bay Area. But the park is still there, and the people are still there. So, for me, that's a success. And when people see that, hopefully, they'll have empathy for the people under freeways and tents, and why can't our public spaces house them and force us to be empathetic? The image on the left is Lafayette

Square Park today. The image on the right is 1906, Golden Gate Park after the earthquake. Why do we have to have cataclysmic events to be empathetic? Our fellow men are out there starving, women sleeping on the street, and we don't see them. Put them in those spaces, and they'll be visible.

And to show you that there are still people out there with empathy, the Oakland Raiders' Bruce Irvin fries' fish every Friday afternoon for anyone who wants it. And by going to that park, that park became the vehicle for him.

The traditional belongs to all of us, and this is a simple one. You go into some neighborhoods -- beautiful architecture, beautiful parks -- but if people look a different way, it's not traditional. It's not until they leave and then new people come in where the traditional gets valued.

A little quick story here: 1888 opera house, the oldest in San Francisco, sits in Bayview–Hunters Point. Over its history, it's provided theater, places for businesses, places for community gatherings, etc. It's also a place where Ruth

Williams taught many black actors. Think: Danny Glover -- came from this place. But over time, with our 1980s federal practices, a lot of these community institutions fell into disrepair. With the San Francisco Arts Council, we were able to raise money and to actually refurbish the place. And we were able to have a community meeting. And within the community meeting, people got up and said, "This place feels like a plantation. Why are we locked in? Why can't we learn theater?" Over the years, people had started putting in chicken coops, hay bales, community gardens and all of these things, and they could not see that traditional thing behind them. But we said, we're bringing the community back. American Disability Act -- we were able to get five million dollars. And now, the tradition belongs to these brown and black people, and they use it. And they learn theater, after-school programs. There're no more chickens. But there is art.

And lastly, I want to share with you a project that we're currently working on, and I think it will force us all to remember in a really different way. There are lots of things in the landscape around us, and most of the time we don't know what's below the ground. Here in Charleston, South Carolina, a verdant piece of grass. Most people just pass by it daily. But underneath it, it's where they discovered Gadsden's Wharf. We think more than 40 percent of the African diaspora landed here. How could you forget that? How could you forget? So, we dug, dug, and we found the wharf. And so, in 2020, Harry Cobb and myself and others are building the International African American Museum.

this place where we know, beneath the ground, thousands died, perished, the food chain of the bay changed. Sharks came closer to the bay. It's where slaves were stored. Imagine this hallowed ground.

So, in this new design, the ground will erupt, and it will talk about this tension that sits below. The columns and the ground are made of tabby shales scooped up from the Atlantic, a reminder of that awful crossing. And as you make your way through on the other side, you are forced to walk through the remains of the warehouse, where slaves were stored on hot, sultry days, for days, and perished. And you'll have to come face-to-face with the Negro, who worked in the marshes, who was able to, with the sickle-cell trait, able to stand in high waters for long, long days. And at night, it'll be open 24/7, for everybody to experience.

But we'll also talk about those other beautiful things that my African ancestors brought with them: a love of landscape, a respect for the spirits that live in trees and rocks and water, the ethnobotanical aspects, the plants that we use for medicinal purposes. But more importantly, we want to remind people in Charleston, South Carolina, of the black bodies, because when you go to Charleston today, the Confederacy is celebrated, probably more than any other city, and you don't have a sense of blackness at all.

The Brookes map, which was an image that helped abolitionists see and be merciful for that condition of the crossing, is something that we want to repeat. And I was taken by the conceptuality of this kind of digital print that sits in a museum in

Charleston. So, we decided to bring the water up on top of the surface, seven feet above tide, and then cast the figures full length, six feet, multiply them across the surface, in tabby, and then allow people to walk across that divide. And hopefully, as people come, the water will drain out, fill up, drain out and fill up. And you'll be forced to come to terms with that memory of place, that memory of that crossing, that at times seems very lucid and clear, but at other times, forces us again to reconcile the scale. And hopefully, as people move through this landscape every day, unreconciled, they'll remember, and hopefully when we remember, e pluribus unum.

References

1. Henrietta fore: child advocate

2. Howard Rheingold: digital community builder

3. Johanna Figueira: digital marketing consultant

4. Jonathan sacks: Not in God's Name: Confronting Religious Violence. Amazon, 2015

5. Matt Trombley: Maven, teacher, team builder

6. Michael Tubbs: mayor of the city of Stockton, California

7. Pope francis: bishop of Rome.

8. shafak elif: Three Daughters of Eve, amazon, 2017

9. Thomas Abt: Bleeding Out: The Devastating Consequences of Urban Violence--and a Bold New Plan for Peace in the Streets, amazon 2019

10. Walter hood: creative director

www.ingramcontent.com/pod-product-compliance
Lightning Source LLC
Chambersburg PA
CBHW061356250726
48657CB00004B/1513